Me and My Self-Image

Copyright

Me and My Self-Image
Author

MEL SILLMON EARNED AN MBA FROM THE UNIVERSITY OF DAYTON AND IS A RETIRED SUPPLY CHAIN EXECUTIVE FROM FORD MOTOR COMPANY. MEL TAUGHT MANY PERSONAL DEVELOPMENT CLASSES AND STRATEGIC MANAGEMENT CLASSES AT THE UNIVERSITY OF MICHIGAN, DEARBORN, AND DETROIT COLLEGE OF BUSINESS. MEL'S DESIRE TO HELP CHILDREN, ADOLESCENTS, AND TEENAGERS TO IMPROVE THEIR SELF-CONFIDENCE AND ESTEEM ORIGINATED FROM HIS PERSONAL EXPERIENCE WITH HIS CHILDREN AND STUDENTS. MEL UTILIZES ILLUSTRATED DYNAMIC VISUALISATIONS AND IMAGERY TO CONVEY THE IMPORTANCE OF FAVORABLE SELF-ESTEEM HABITATS. IT BECAME INCREASINGLY EVIDENT, THROUGH OBSERVATIONS THAT A CHILD'S SELF-IMAGE AND ATTITUDE ARE CRITICAL IN THE DEVELOPMENT OF THEIR POTENTIAL.

Me and My Self-Image

HELLO I AM
SOPHIA

Me and My Self-Image

SOMETIME IT IS UP AND
SOMETIME IT IS DOWN

Me and My Self-Image

MY SELF-IMAGE SEEMS TO ALWAYS COME AROUND

Me and My Self-Image

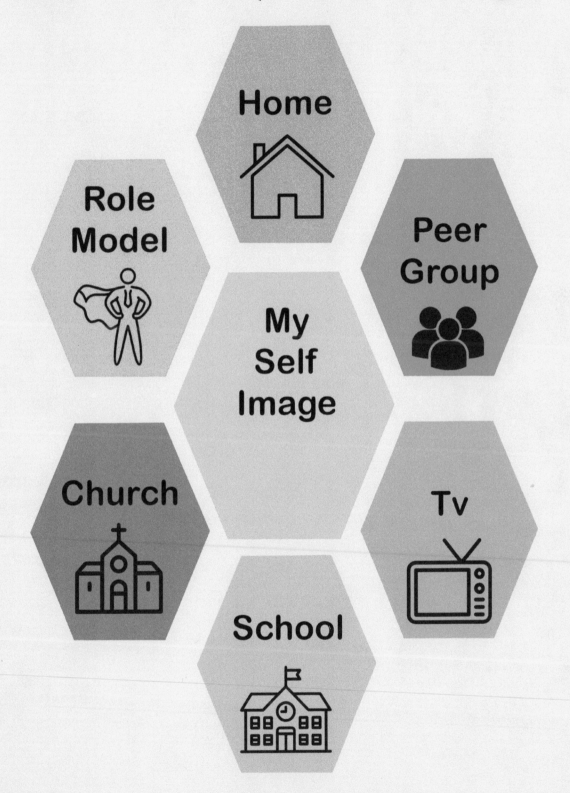

MY SELF-IMAGE IS THE RESULT OF MANY THINGS

Me and My Self-Image

Self-image means you usually feel good about yourself.

I am Confident

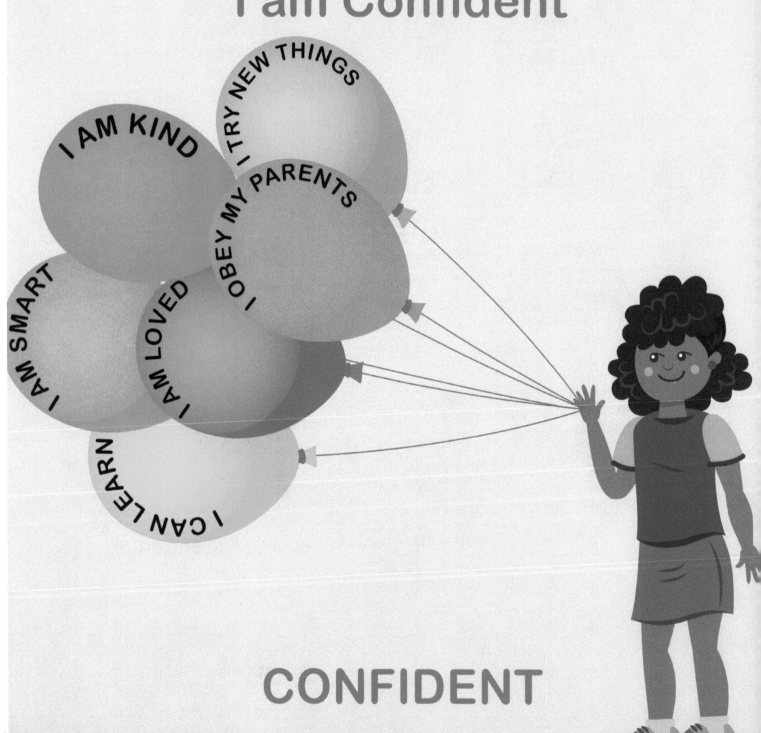

CONFIDENT

Me and My Self-Image

SELF CONFIDENCE PLAN
BELIEVE IN YOURSELF

READ

CREATE

DEVELOP YOUR SKILLS

Me and My Self-Image

MY CONFIDENCE PLAN

LEARN

DEVELOP YOUR SKILLS

Me and My Self-Image

MY ATTITUDE

Me and My Self-Image

YOUR ATTITUDE

ATTITUDE	I CHOOSE MY OWN VIEW POINT
GRADES	I GET GOOD GRADES
MATH	I AM SMART IN MATH

I AM SMART

Me and My Self-Image

I DON'T QUIT

DO IT — I CAN DO IT

SELF TALK — I FOLLOW THE POSITIVE SELF TALK GROUP

SOLUTIONS — EVERY PROBLEM HAS A SOLUTION

YOUR ATTITUDE DETERMINES HOW SUCCESSFUL YOU WILL BE

Me and My Self-Image
Growth Mindset

LIFE IS LIKE RIDING A BICYCLE,
YOU MAY FALL DOWN, GET UP
AND KEEP ON PEDALING

Me and My Self-Image

YOUR ABILITIES ARE IMPROVED
AS YOU BEGAN TO PUSH YOURSELF

WRITING

I AM SMART

HOMEWORK

MATH

SCIENCE

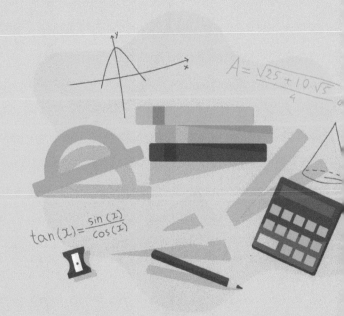

Me and My Self-Image

I CAN'T

Me and My Self-Image

NEGATIVE SELF-TALK

I CAN'T IS A BELIEF THAT YOU CANNOT DO SOMETHING BEFORE YOU TRY

OUR NEGATIVE SELF-TALK

MAY AFFECT OUR EMOTIONS, MOTIVATIONS, AND FUTURE ACTION THAT MAY BE REQUIRED TO ACCOMPLISH OUR GOALS

Me and My Self-Image

Positive Mindset

Me and My Self-Image

Mindzet

BELIEVE
IN
YOURSELF

Me and My Self-Image
Mindset

I CAN
I WILL
I AM SMART

Me and My Self-Image

Image mindset means you usually
Feel good about yourself

Me and My Self-Image

FAMILY VALUES

Me and My Self-Image
THE FORMATION OF YOUR

SELF-IMAGE
MAYBE INFLUENCED
IN PART
BY YOUR
FAMILY VALUES

Me and My Self-Image

FAMILY VALUES AND SELF IMAGE

THINK OF A PERSON

THAT HAS MADE A POSITIVE DIFFERENCE IN YOUR LIFE

Growth Mindset

LIFE IS LIKE RIDING A BICYCLE,
YOU MAY FALL DOWN, GET UP
AND KEEP ON PEDALING

CPSIA information can be obtained
at www.ICGtesting.com
Printed in the USA
BVHW090011011221
622871BV00017B/731